How to have a healthy relationship.

By

Betty B.Miller

How to have a healthy relationship.

TABLE OF CONTENT

Introduction 4

Chapter 1 7

How to pay attention to your spouse 7

Chapter 2 13

Ways to avoid Conflicts in Relationships and Grow Together..13

Chapter 3 18

How to Resolve Relationship Conflicts without Hurting Each Other 18

Chapter 4 25

Ways to Improve Communication in a Relationship 25

Chapter 5 41

Ways to Show Appreciation to the Love of Your Life. ..41

Chapter 6 51

30 Signs you're With the Right Person 51

Chapter 7 68

What Your Body Language Says About Your Relationship..68

Conclusion..75

Introduction

Relationships are like flowers that grow in full swing when nourished with love and care. We desire intimacy and love. We desire meaningful interactions, we crave delight and pride anytime we see our spouse doing what we enjoy.

The relationship may occasionally lose its spark. lovers might lose the passion they felt for one another while they were dating. A day would come and they would be joyful or depressed it might make you wonder whether your spouse is the perfect one for you. Regular communication is the cornerstone of any relationship, it keeps the connection together and when communication is lacking in the relationship, it scatters the relationship. It even scatters the most ideal couples. Therefore, a relationship must have solid communication abilities.You are fortunate since we are going to speak about the keys to healthy communication in your relationship. We would also learn how to avoid disputes and how to settle them.

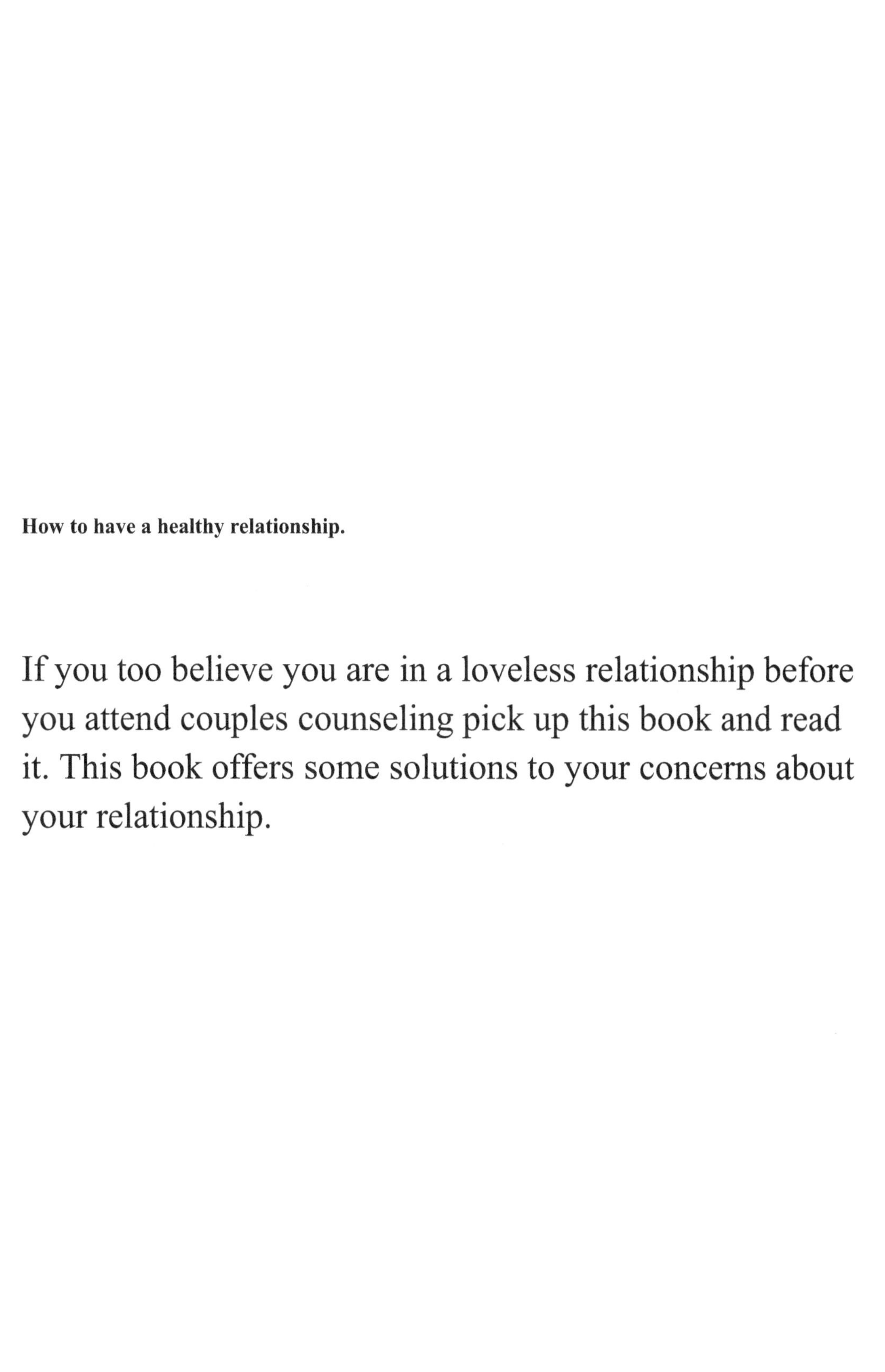

How to have a healthy relationship.

If you too believe you are in a loveless relationship before you attend couples counseling pick up this book and read it. This book offers some solutions to your concerns about your relationship.

Chapter 1

How to pay attention to your spouse

We all desire attentive spouses. I'm not talking about clingy partners, but rather the sort that recognizes when we're not feeling well or recalls the names of our family members. There are some fairly straightforward methods to be a more attentive spouse if that's something you're trying to improve upon in your relationship. After all, there's nothing worse than having a spouse who comes and leaves when they want sex, then spends the rest of their time with their friends, or watching TV, and who hardly recognizes you're alive. That's not a loving, life-affirming connection. Whether you've been in a relationship for a long, it's never too late to master these loving, passionate, crucial relationship skills.

1. Get off Your Phone

Nothing screams "I'm only half listening" like being on your phone while someone's attempting to chat with you. Just make a deliberate effort to put your phone aside anytime you are giving your spouse your attention.

Even if your spouse isn't attempting to speak to you like if you're watching a movie, putting your phone aside gives the message that you're present in the moment.

2. Be A Good Social Media Friend

Like those Instagram pictures. Comment on the rare Facebook post. Retweet the clever Tweets. It may sound ridiculous, but it will show your spouse that you care, that you think they're hilarious, that you appreciate seeing their selfies, that you're prepared to perform online PDA (to a degree), and that you're happy with your partner. It is tempting to go overboard, but you may simply ask your spouse how they feel about their degree of social media attention.

3. Learn How to pay attention

Listening is more than consideration. It's body language, head nodding, asking questions, paying attention (not being on your phone), and demonstrating you are involved in the discussion. Then, it's taking what you heard one step further and acting on your discussion. Being a good listener may change an ordinary relationship into a terrific one.

4. Ask Questions

Asking questions is a simple approach to being more attentive. Ask your spouse about their day. Ask if they need anything as you get up to walk to the kitchen. Inquire how they're feeling. Ask how their clubs or occupations are doing. Ask whether they spoke to their relatives. Just ask questions that indicate you're paying attention and that you're interested in their life.

5. Make Note of What's Going On In Their Lives

You should remember the name of that individual at work who usually gives them a hard time. You should know what they despise about their commute. You should know what dog park they enjoy going to. You should make it your duty to take an active interest in the day-to-day. It's the simple things that frequently begin to build distance in a relationship.

6. Do More Things Together

If you're a gym rat, but your partner's a city runner, choose a day when they run with you and you go to the gym with them. See if you can sneak lunch dates into your day.

The more time you spend together, the more possibilities you have to be attentive, show interest, be loving, and get to know your spouse even better.

7. Make Little Routines

Talk during your lunch break. Text each other to have a fantastic day and discuss your commute home. Send each other YouTube videos of love songs during your coffee break. Just select a few basic methods to demonstrate love, and do them every single day, without fail. My "good morning gorgeous" messages are one of my favorite parts of every single day. It's something extremely basic yet incredibly important.

8. Get into Their Interests

If you extreme dislike sports, you don't have to unexpectedly turn into a fan, but you might find it pleasurable to go to a game as one or to host a tailgate party. If there's a show they like, watch it too, so you can have a discussion about it. Study about what they care for so you can ask questions or get them stuffs they might want. It will go a long way to help your partner feel known and understood.

9. Purchase Them Specific Gifts

Take your careful thought to their interests' one step more and present them with a gift that lets them recognize you support their happiness. For example, if you normally buy flowers, this time get paints and brushes for your art-loving partner or get potted succulents for your garden-loving partner. Those types of gifts are as passionate as they are considerate.

10. Pay Attention to Their Body

Listen to their breathing and pay attention to their body motions as you have sex. Observe when they get a hairdo. Pitch in a bit extra when you see they're feeling fatigued or ill. Show attention and concern when they limp. Have a delicate and sensitive consideration for their emotions and physique.

11. Remember Special Events

There's no excuse for forgetting anniversaries, birthdays, and special occasions. You can set the dates into your mobile phone and get loads of reminders.

How to have a healthy relationship.

Go one step beyond and include in important other events, like a year at their employment, the anniversary of when you acquired your first place or their favorite pet's anniversary

Master these things, as well as some decent communication skills and some healthy trust, and you'll bc a shoo-in for a partner of the year.

Chapter 2

Ways to avoid Conflicts in Relationships and Grow Together

Interpersonal conflict happens when expectations aren't being fulfilled. Each individual gets into a relationship with specific expectations. These are based on prior experiences, upbringing, or how you believe things should be.

The difficulty is that no two individuals think the same, no matter how much you have in common.

A lot of couples perceive disagreement as an opportunity to bail either because they were previously searching for a route out or because they panic and feel threatened. When our ego feels threatened, it triggers our flight-or-fight reaction. Sometimes it may be hard to find a settlement on a problem, making issues worse.

Instead of perceiving conflict as a danger to a relationship, what if we reframed this and viewed the conflict as an opportunity and a sign of progress in a partnership?

This entails knowing that conflict will eventually arise in a close relationship. The only way of getting around that is to not voice your views at all, this is not healthy.

So what if we concentrated on productively expressing our thoughts?

To accomplish this:

1. Remember not to sweat the minor things.

Instead of making every small molehill a mountain, vow to not make everything a war until it's vital. Realize that not every disagreement has to be an argument. Of course, this doesn't mean you succumb to someone else's demands when it's something you feel passionately about, but take the time to analyze the amount of significance of the topic at hand.

2. Practice acceptance.

If you find yourself in the thick of a fight, try to remember that the other person is coming into the scene with an entirely different history and sct of experiences than yourself.

You have not been in this person's shoes, and although it may help to attempt to put yourself in them, your partner is the only one who can fully understand where he or she is coming from.

3. Exercise patience.

Granted, it's hard to remember this in the heat of the moment. But pausing to take a few deep breaths, and resolving to take a break and return to the issue when emotions are not as high, might sometimes be the best approach to cope with the present problem.

4. Lower your expectations.

This is not to imply you should have low expectations but it is to say that you should bear in mind you may have different expectations. The easiest method to convey this is to inquire what another's expectations are in a circumstance. Again, don't instantly assume that you come into the scenario with the same expectations.

But what if you are in the middle of a fight and you don't appear to be accomplishing anything other than polarizing each other?

5. Remember you both wish for harmony.

Most likely, you both want to get back on track and enjoy a pleasant relationship. Also, recall the sensation of togetherness that you desire to experience. It's impossible to feel intimidated by someone when you perceive yourself as related and striving for the same purpose.

6. Focus on the other person's conduct, not their attributes.

Personal assaults may be significantly more harmful and long-lasting. Talk about what actions disturbed you instead of what is "wrong" with someone's nature.

7. Clarify what the individual intended by their conduct instead of what you took their action to signify.

Most of the time, your spouse is not actively intending to injure you, and being wounded occurred to be a result of that activity.

8. Keep in mind your purpose is to solve the issue rather than win the battle.

Resist the impulse to be contrarian solely for that reason. Remember that it's better to be happy than correct!

9. Accept the other person's reaction.

Once you have communicated your thoughts as to what a person's actions meant to you, accept their reply. If they tell you the intended meaning of their conduct was not how you perceived it, accept it at face value.

Once you've both had the chance to tell your side, mutually agree to let it go. In the best-case scenario, your talk will finish in a mutually pleasant manner. If it doesn't, you may opt to revisit it later. When making this choice, ask yourself how essential it is to you. If you choose to leave it in the past, try your best to accomplish so, rather than bringing it up again in future disagreements.

Conflict may be stressful. If you perceive it as a chance for progress, it might help you get closer and strengthen your relationship.

Chapter 3

How to Resolve Relationship Conflicts without Hurting Each Other

Relationship discord impacts even the happiest marriages. But how can you conclude an argument when you simply can't seem to agree?

It can feel devastating and total provoking when you feel like your spouse isn't listening to you. Many couples make the error of attempting to speak over one othcr instead of talking to each other during a marital disagreement.

But genuine communication isn't about who can scream the loudest or who can receive pot-shots at the other. It's about resolving a matter at hand.

• What causes relationship disagreement?

• How do you handle disagreement in a relationship?

How you manage a quarrel reveals a lot about how you feel about your relationship.

That's why we're looking at 9 polite methods you may handle marital disputes without generating a wedge between you and your spouse.

1. Don't Yell – Communicate

Communication is the cornerstone of healthy, successful partnerships.

Partners who converse with one another establish a feeling of trust. They understand how the other one thinks and feels and understands what triggers to avoid.

Communicate with your spouse often — even if you're disagreeing. When things grow hot, it might be tough to retain your cool. If you want to handle marital disagreement without harming your spouse, avoid shouting and name-calling.

Speak to solve by asking questions such as:

• Who are you furious with?

• What is at the base of the problem?

• How can you settle the conflict?

• How can you avoid this problem from coming up again in the future?

2. Learn to Listen

Listening is equally as crucial as talking when it comes to dispute resolution. You show your spouse decency when you hear what they have to say. It would also be advisable to keep silent and patient while your spouse conveys their opinion. You may also handle relationship issues gently by avoiding distractions. Maintain eye contact while you communicate, and remove distractions such as the television, radio, or phone.

3. Choose the Right Time to Bring up Differences

If you have a matter you want to set right with your other half, it’s significant to choose the right moment to bring it up. Problem-solving will go easier if your partner is aware and in a good mood.

But bringing up a topic that might lead to an argument would not be appropriate if they are irritable, fatigued, stressed out, hungry, or preoccupied.

4. Watch Your Tone

Do you comprehend your tone of voice?

We may believe we are expressing something in a light way to our spouse only to have them break into tears, certain that we are shouting at them. If you want to handle marital problems without harming your spouse, avoid employing sarcasm or disparaging tones.

Arguing over text is a sure-fire method to be misinterpreted by your spouse. Your partner is left wondering what tone you're speaking to them with.

If you believe that you're being misinterpreted through text message, contact your spouse and straighten things out immediately.

5. Show Respect

When things get intense, you may resort to some rude words or actions that you usually wouldn't.

Disrespecting your spouse is one of the most horrible things you can do through a disagreement.

You can resolve relationship difference without hurting your other half by taking a minute to settle down. Disagreement resolution isn't about seeing who can shout the loudest or opening old wound to make your spouse surrender. It's about solving a crisis.

Show value to your equal through disagreements by:

- Sticking to the matter at hand
- pleasing your spouse's opinions critically
- Not interrupting your other half
- Listening tolerantly
- Letting calmer minds prevail

6. Remember That You Love Each Other

We tend to get carried away when we are furious, but it's crucial to remember that the person you are fighting with is also the love of your life. Not even the happiest couples agree on every topic. It's alright to have arguments once in a while so long as you treat each other with love and respect when you do. Don't snooze on a dispute. You never know what tomorrow will bring, so why not makeup and give yourself a nice night's sleep?

7. Have Empathy

Misunderstandings erupt into conflicts when spouses don't grasp where the other person is coming from. That is when empathy comes into play.

Empathy is the capacity to comprehend someone else's emotions. When you have empathy for your partner you're able to put yourself in their shoes and view things from their perspective.

Having empathy is key to resolving interpersonal difficulties calmly. When you empathize with your partner, you are giving them your attention, bridging the difference in your dispute, and developing compassion.

8. Agree to Disagree

Whether it's about politics, religion, or families, there are going to be certain moments when you and your spouse just can't agree. In these cases, it's better to agree to disagree. This indicates that you both realize that neither will sway the other's view on an issue.

So long as the subject at hand is not urgent and will not significantly affect your family relationships, such as bad financial choices or concerns involving, just agree to disagree and move on.

9. Learn to Forgive

One method you may prevent hurting your spouse's emotions during a marital disagreement is by learning how to forgive them. It's simple to say you forgive someone, but forgiveness is more than your words.

You demonstrate you forgive someone when you let the subject drop - not using it as leverage in a future dispute.

True forgiveness is letting go of the anger you feel and treating your spouse with love and respect when the fight is done.

Chapter 4

Ways to Improve Communication in a Relationship

Why is communication crucial in a relationship? Healthy communication in a relationship establishes a basis of enduring trust, satisfaction, and openness between partners. Communication is one of the important factors in a good relationship.

Why communication fails

You and your spouse will confront communication challenges at some time. Over time, people have difficulties getting through to one another. Emotions get in the way, the connection is aggravating, communication walls build up, and before you realize it, a point is reached when you prefer not to communicate. Fortunately, communication is a very straightforward repair but does need time.

Since communication in partnerships is a big part of our day-to-day lives, it is important in a relationship.

Signs you need to improve communication. Sometimes, it might be hard to comprehend why things aren't healing despite the dialogue that has been going place. It might be thus because probably the excellent communication skills in a relationship are absent.

The appropriate communication may assist produce outstanding relationship outcomes and make the partnership healthy. But how can you know about the signals you need to strengthen communication? Check out these 5 indications to advise you:

- **One way communication**

One way of communication is when you are the only one speaking in the discussion without allowing the other person to give their perspective. Observe whether your communication is one-way. It is one of the indicators that you should sit back and listen to your companion.

- **Negative talks**

Does either of you engage more in criticizing each other rather than successfully communicating? Avoid talking badly since this will not lead to any effect.

- **Disrespecting emotions**

If one of you is invalidating the other person's emotions, this is one of the indicators you need to enhance communication. Avoid stating something like, "I don't care."

- **'You' statements**

If your statement starts with 'you', this shows you have inadequate communication skills. It suggests that you are more drawn towards blaming your spouse than seeking a solution.

- **Getting personal**

One of the signals you both need to enhance your communication is when one of you believes that personal assaults are being made in the course of conversing. Avoid targeting each other's weaknesses.

What good communication truly implies

Being in love implies you both will be able to speak pretty readily, which is equally crucial since, without communication, the relationship would have no possibility of survival.

Effective communication is when it incorporates two elements:

- Speaking
- Listening

It may seem simple, but it takes considerable practice. Again, when speaking, you need to remember the aspects of speaking in truth and love. While you are listening, ensure that you are actively listening, comprehending, and expressing empathy.

In good communication, several degrees are beginning with cliché and end with giving opinions without any reservations. Know about these below:

20 methods to increase communication in your relationships

How to increase communication in a relationship? Here are some communication methods and advice on enhancing communication in a relationship.

1. Break down communication hurdles: Establish an open communication connection. There is no space for walls when it comes to communicating in partnerships.

Good communication demands transparency. The fact is, barriers are not broken simply because you wish them to go away. They don't evaporate when you tell someone, "I want to tear down our communication barriers."

One of the strategies to increase communication in a relationship involves obstacles to be torn down via gradual transformation. When it comes to communication hurdles in relationships, start by eliminating the criticism, blame, and/or defensiveness from verbal encounters.

Openness only happens when both people feel comfortable and secure.

2. Stay in the present

One guaranteed method to anger someone is to bring up the past. When anything causes a negative reaction, it is a cue to cease. Communication in partnerships must stay in the present since living in the past adversely impacts the present.

As one of the strategies to increase communication in a relationship, keep each discussion, including the unpleasant ones, calm and courteous by concentrating on the issue at hand.

Referencing the past easily escalates simple disputes into enormous fights. Before you know it, utterly unneeded things are uttered, and the relationship takes a blow.

There is no need to escalate anything simple.

3. Listen more than you talk

How to increase relationship communication?

Another on the list of vital strategies to enhance communication in a relationship is to understand the value of listening more than you talk.

If you take the time to hear and digest what the other person is saying, you will have a deeper grasp of their perspective and they will understand you by doing the same. In the excitement of the moment, we tend to pick on tiny fragments of what someone is saying but entirely miss the overall picture. This is the source of individuals feeling misunderstood and as we know, misconceptions lead to irritation and develop walls that are hard to break through. To apply this suggestion, offer talks more structure by avoiding interrupting and concentrating more on what a person is saying rather than what you intend to say next.

4. Watch nonverbal signals

Nonverbal communication is equally as, if not more, vital than verbal communication. Work on communication in a relationship through the use of body language. Our body language and gestures speak it all.

A few examples would include crossed arms, evidence of being closed off or feeling attacked, placing the body away, an indicator of defensiveness and a lack of eye contact, and a symptom of either dishonesty or indifference. Pay attentive attention to the person you are talking to. Good communication is like a dance that needs both parties to receive signals from one another. If you are getting the impression that you should back off or steer a discussion elsewhere, heed the signal.

When two individuals can read each other, they get closer because a mutual understanding of limits is developed.

5. Never underestimate the effect of honesty

Communicating freely and honestly is one of the keys to developing the connection.

Communication in partnerships depends significantly on honesty. One of the relationship communication skills and techniques to increase communication in a relationship is to develop is keeping honesty in communication in a partnership. Honesty does not simply mean stating the truth. It also entails being honest with oneself about your thoughts and ideas. One of the strategies to strengthen communication is to be authentic. Establishing communication in a relationship implies building a connection where communication is not a problem in the first place, and both parties work at adopting effective strategies to communicate better.

6. Timing is everything

Along with adopting the ideas for better communication or how to communicate better in a relationship, don’t forget about time. Timing plays a significant part when it comes to fostering effective communication in a relationship, as inappropriate talk and wrong tone may wreak havoc on marital happiness.

7. Always speak face to face

Slightly relevant subjects must be addressed face to face. A face-to-face talk is one of the most efficient means of communicating in a relationship.

Phone conversations, messages, and emails merely create loose ends as sometimes they might be ambiguous. It is easy to misread what someone is saying, particularly in messages and emails. These types of interpersonal communication have a role but having meaningful talks isn't one of them.

8. Wait a day or two

When unhappy over anything, of course, you want to make your sentiments known. So, how to communicate effectively about the gap or dispute in the relationship with your spouse? Well, certainly do that, but take one or two days to calm down and analyze the scenario through.

So, how do communicate properly in a relationship?

Even when the urge is great, wait. You want to be the one to talk, not your rage. Anger in relationships comprises nothing except nasty and accusing rhetoric.

Ways to increase communication in a relationship include implementing a 24-hour rule.

Here's some short and simple advice on acing the art of communicating in a relationship. If an oversight on your lover's part won't matter after 24 hours, then letting go of expressing issues is the greatest path to promoting improved communication in a relationship.

9. Understand your own emotions

It is only normal to want to address a problem immediately when it arises, but you need time to encourage successful communication in a relationship. Before you begin to talk with your significant other, be clear about your emotions.

Sit for a time and digest what's going on in your mind. Emotional awareness helps cleanse your brain and converse better. You may accomplish that by examining your feelings and maintaining a journal of how you feel each day.

10. Use 'I' statements

Ways to build that comfort and safety include avoiding beginning sentences with the extremely accusatory "you," start expressing sentiments with "I feel" or "I am," and making requests by opening with, "Can you" or "I would appreciate it if you." "I" words in talks assist your partner to comprehend your sentiments. Such remarks show your strong sentiments about the issue and assist your spouse to comprehend your choices.

Some of the instances of "I" utterances are:

- I feel lonely when you leave the dinner table.
- I feel uneasy when you speak about my past.
- I feel disturbed when you don't tell me your troubles.

11. Set a goal to resolve

Unless the main purpose of initiating the discussion is to achieve a solution or a conclusion, it won't do you both any good and merely add to the already existing misery. So, make a goal to settle the situation before you begin the dialogue. Once you have the objective in sight, both of you will not divert from the purpose.

12. Establish boundaries

In a relationship, it is vital to draw boundaries. It informs the spouses how they would desire to be treated by each other. It also makes obvious the personal values that they would wish to safeguard. Spouses may accomplish that by asking for permission, being honest, and showing respect when differences in beliefs come to light.

13. Avoid shouting

Screaming and screaming will lead to no good. It will just lead to more anxious talks. So, converse gently, and in circumstances when your spouse starts to blame you for anything, terminate the discussion instead of becoming furious and yelling back. If necessary, publicly ask for a break. Here, it becomes your obligation to psychologically appraise the scenario.

14. Leave love notes

Sometimes, printed words will accomplish more magic than face-to-face interactions. So, as one of the main techniques to increase communication in a relationship, remember to leave beautiful notes for your lover in their most frequented areas. It might be inside the closet, inside the automobile refrigerator door, etc.

You may write generic love-filled words, apologize for any of your previous misdeeds, or hint at them about the sex plans.

15. Don't be sarcastic

Don't be snarky or condescending in the relationship. This will demonstrate you have unpleasant sentiments toward your spouse, and this will only hurt the relationship. While amusing repartees are usually appreciated, crossing the line will lead to insult jokes. Partners should observe their behaviors and wait for a time to find acceptable words when they like to make a snarky remarks.

16. Pick the proper spot

You must resolve communication issues in privacy and the comfort of your home. In cases of issues, avoid fighting in public or at social events. If you both feel a surge of anger, avoid talking in public and wait till you both reach home.

This will also buy you both some time to calm down.

17. Understand your partner's needs

Most difficulties emerge because couples fail to comprehend one other's needs. You both need to watch closely and guarantee the requirements of both parties are given regard. This may happen with calm dialogue and create relationship pleasure.

18. Don't interrupt

When you want to have a conversation, do not begin merely because you want to chat. Don't interrupt your spouse or expect them to abandon their present work to converse.

Rather, ask if they have a minute or if the two of you may chat later. Initiating a discussion with an interruption adds an unneeded annoyance right from the outset.

19. Send pleasant remarks

As one of the important techniques to increase communication in a relationship, it is crucial to let the other person know you are invested in the discussion. It will inspire children to express themselves freely. You might nod your head in moments of agreement or grin from time to time to demonstrate your interest.

20. Respond rather than react

Responding entails the thought of the consequence of the dialogue and incorporates emotional intelligence. However, responding may have both good and bad implications and is dependent solely on emotions.

Last but not least, in the list of strategies to enhance communication in a relationship, remember not to respond to everything your spouse says immediately. You must reply to their difficulties calmly and gently.

To learn how to successfully communicate, remember that the appropriate communication skills may do wonders in making the connection easier and healthier. It will give a lot of transparency to the relationship you have with each other as well.

So, learn to speak with your spouse by practicing effective communication in relationships and creating a deeper love link, trust, and empathy in a relationship.

Chapter 5

Ways to Show Appreciation to the Love of Your Life.

We all get pulled in a million different ways and, therefore, forget about the significance of being able to express gratitude for the love of our life. If you're like most people who are over-committed and attempting to continually mark things off your "to-do list," take time to sit down and appreciate the person who loves you by reminding them how important they are to you.

Your spouse just isn't a priority. Though we appreciate them, we also have a propensity to take them for granted, and here is when a relationship may go down the wrong road.

Making a deliberate effort to express a little gratitude or showering words of appreciation on a loved one may go a long way!

You need to discover easy methods to express gratitude to your mate and learn how to show someone you love them without words. After all, tiny efforts may make a tremendous impact.

8 methods of valuing love

This is the person you have pledged your life to, which demonstrates you love them every day. Sure, they have their times as we all do, but this is the person who genuinely is the love of your life and so you want to demonstrate your love and respect, and just how important they are to you.

This doesn't need to be something complex or costly, because often the tiniest mementos may serve to express thanks in a very large manner. It's all about thinking through what they enjoy, what makes them happy, and what will allow them to feel significant and appreciated after everything is said and done.

So, how do demonstrate gratitude in relationships? Here are some easy yet powerful ways to tell you to appreciate someone!

1. Do something for them for no reason at all

You don't need a specific occasion to do something kind for them.

It also doesn't need to be something extravagant, because it may be as simple as a card or giving them a massage. The crucial aspect here is to take the time out to do something simply for them, for no reason at all, and with no strings attached. You aren't doing this to obtain something yourself, but rather to encourage them to feel loved in a basic yet profound manner.

The tiny things will aid to put a smile on their face, and they will feel valued for being appreciated in a relationship, all because of these simple signs of appreciation in partnerships.

2. Cook their favorite food

One of the ways to demonstrate gratitude in a relationship is by cooking for your significant other. What a simple idea to appreciate the love!

Cook their favorite supper so that they are surprised when they arrive home and it's ready for them. This is probably one of the nicest methods to express thanks to your mate. Pack their lunch for them one day out of the blue, or even try to surprise them with breakfast in bed.

The road to the heart is via the stomach and preparing them a favorite meal is guaranteed to make them feel appreciated and fuel their body and spirit. Appreciation in relationships comes from simple things, and preparing their favorite food is simply one way to express it. In addition, this is how to show an important person you care for without words.

3. Send them a text to convey them your love and admiration

How to praise someone you love without burning a hole in your pocket? Send them a love-filled message. Appreciating an important person you love doesn't get easier than this. There's nothing better than a surprise SMS in the middle of the day to make you grin.

If you want to express gratitude in relationships to the love of your life, then send them a brief text during a hectic workday, merely to let them know you're thinking of them and that you love them. Phrases like, "I love you and value you," or a simple one-liner like, "I value you," can do wonders. It's unexpected, and it's simple, yet those few words may mean so much.

You may also look for love appreciation quotes or admire your lover's quotes on the internet and share them with them to catch them off guard. You will feel thrilled when you catch them grinning when they see you later on again, the small things count so much when it comes to displaying gratitude in relationships!

4. Give them the day off from duties

We all get caught up in all the things we have to do, and sometimes simply giving people a day off to rest may work wonders. Nothing can work better than this - freeing them from their chores, even if it is only for a single day, is one of the finest methods to express gratitude in relationships that matter so much to you.

Tell them that it's their day to rest, and you take over their chores around the home.

Do the groceries shopping, clean the home, mow the grass, or do anything so that they don't have to. Allow them time to sleep in and relax and show them that you are doing this because you appreciate everything that they do for you. It's one day, and while it involves extra effort for you, it will go a long way in enabling them to feel sincerely appreciated.

Telling someone you appreciate them does not need your words or goods. Kind gestures like the one discussed above may say volumes of how much they mean to you and that they are cherished for who they are.

5. Pamper them and set the tone for a day of love

Nothing can enable a person to feel valued quite like a day of pampering! If you are low on cash, then set yourself a spa day at home. Women just love to feel pampered, and this is one of the nicest ways to express thanks. If you adore your wife, simply pamper them a lot. That's the deception!

Draw them a bath, lay up candles, prepare them a delicious meal, and give them a massage. Everyone loves to be taken care of once in a while, and this goes a long way in allowing them time to decompress and think about how much they mean to you in the process.

So, how do you understand someone? Simply! Send them to a health spa.

6. Thank them

Show your thanks by telling them how essential they are to you as frequently as possible. Looking for the appropriate phrases to communicate love and appreciation?

It might be anything as basic as saying “I love you” that goes the farthest. Remind them via your words how important they are to you, and tell them face to face how much you care.

Having an open and direct channel of contact means that you get to communicate with them what they mean to you all the time. So just remember to do this and to utter your words of thanks and that may be all that it takes in the end.

7. Show love

Showing gratitude in a relationship goes a long way in establishing your love connection. So, how to express gratitude in a relationship?

As mentioned previously, appreciating your girlfriend or spouse requires no terms or gifts. Just cling onto them in that embrace a bit longer. Kiss a bit deeper, and look them in the eyes with the love that you have. Sometimes you do have to truly demonstrate your gratitude via compassion and love. And, this is one of the greatest responses to the topic, of how to appreciate your sweetheart. When you can gaze them in the eyes and make physical understanding and that bond a true priority, then you are telling them all that they require to know. Though life gets hectic, working to keep that connection and physical bond strong will make sure that they know how you think and demonstrate it to them without speaking any words at all.

It is vital to be grateful for those who love you and stand by you through thick and thin to weather the storms as one. So, be trained how to show admiration without saying something.

8. Speak to them; remind them why you feel affection for them

On how to show admiration to your spouse, the best tip is to be thankful for your loved ones and assist them by supporting them. Being present for someone that you love is frequently one of the finest ways to demonstrate gratitude in relationships.

Help them through anything or simply listen to them when they need you. Though it's always good to express thanks to the love of your life in unique ways, it may also be about returning to basics when it comes to displaying love and appreciation.

Men, appreciate your girlfriend vocally as much as you can because ladies adore hearing about it. Women, don't only be captivated by this, do reciprocate. So, how to tell someone how much you value them? Remind them why you love them, remind them that you are there for them, and aid to support them when they need a small boost.

When someone understands that they can depend on you, then it's the greatest praise, and it helps to build somebody up when they need it.

A modest gesture may go a long way, and the gratitude will always be repaid too!

This will be one of the best ways to show appreciation in relationships. For every relationship, gratitude is one of the utmost mantras. A relationship runs on efforts and gratitude. Once you begin understanding your spouse’s contribution to your life and make sure that you acknowledge them and appreciate them, your relationship is sure to flourish.

Chapter 6

30 Signs you're With the Right Person

The simple question "Am I with the appropriate person?" indicates that, on some level, you're having second opinion it'd be so lovely to get solid response and know, without a shadow of a doubt, that your spouse is "the one." Unfortunately, there's not a gigantic green flag floating over your partner's head when you first meet them, urging you to pursue the connection. But because life and relationships are seldom so clear, questions and fears are likely to surface. It's typical for spouses in long-term relationships to face misgivings at some time. it doesn't always indicate you're headed for a split. You'll probably encounter periods of ambivalence, boredom, and even uncertainty. This is particularly true if you have a history of unhealthy relationships. It's crucial to evaluate whether you're letting prior unpleasant events overwhelm your present relationship, take time to speak to your spouse about anxieties, and seek treatment to help you overcome your past. This way you may have a healthy and happy relationship.

Reassessing the pros and drawbacks (even if there aren't too many) of your relationship is quite essential, as it might help you figure out whether you're suited for each other in the long term. Do you still connect as well as you did in the beginning on problems, ideas, and lifestyles? Do you envision yourself still with them in the next five years as you seek career and personal growth? it's useful to reassess what's important to you as well as what makes the connection seem unique. If you discover someone who still satisfies your relationship expectations even after being together for a long, then that may be the appropriate person. Being in a relationship where you can find a compromise to each partner's expectations is vital for developing a firm foundation.

So, wondering how to tell whether you're with the correct person? Here are 30 indicators you are, even if you've doubted your relationship.

1. It's Easy To Be Around Them

One of the most crucial sensations to look for, while judging whether a relationship is good for you, is comfort.

If you have a sense of comfort in being with this person, you're not frequently on edge, hyper-vigilant, ready for a conflict, or feel ignored which is a positive sign It doesn't mean you won't have occasional disputes or times of strain. It merely means the whole feeling is calm and natural.

2. You Can Be Yourself in the Relationship

Branching off of that, you realize it's OK to be yourself. You feel free to express what's on your mind, bring up challenging issues, and let your hair down because you know they won't pass judgment or love you any less. "Bending to impress a person or your relationship is never a good idea. Showing your genuine colors from the beginning is a vital element of a good and healthy relationship. This also means they approach with compassion and understanding even when you aren't at your best, like when you're unwell, in a foul mood, or walled off because you're going through a stressful period.

3. Your Personalities Are Complementary

They say opposites attract, but occasionally a genuinely excellent match may be discovered in someone who compliments you. So take a minute to examine. Are they extroverted, while you're reserved? Are they thoughtful, while you're fast to discover answers to problems? You're likely dating the appropriate person if your differences add balance to each other's life

4. You Share the Same Values

Do you share comparable worldviews and have similar opinions, morals, values, and beliefs? If so, you're on the correct course. While having hobbies and interests is fantastic, these things are so much more essential since they imply you're moving on the same path in life.

5. You Stay On the Same "Team" When Arguing

Relationships tend to break apart when partners regard each other as adversaries during fights, instead of finding ways to remain on the same side even when they're both really upset. If you and your partner are a good fit, you'll notice that you work through disagreements, speak about your issues, listen, and achieve a resolution.

You debate, but it never turns vicious. And more significantly, you always come out on the other side with new limits and greater knowledge of one another.

6. You know they're Loyal

Think about how it feels when you call and your lover doesn't answer or send an SMS and they don't respond or they get home late from work. Do you anticipate the worst? If you can readily trust each other in everything you do, this implies you are comfortable with each other. While prior relationship experience might factor into how easy it is to trust a partner, you're likely with the correct person if they're open and honest and eager to do whatever it takes to create trust in your relationship.

7. You Hear Each Other

What this effectively implies is that, when you communicate your problems, your spouse truly listens. Listening to each other also avoids tiny difficulties from becoming major ones, which is vital if you want to remain together.

8. You can't determine what is wrong

Thoughts profoundly impact how we perceive the behavior of others and our expectations. So, take a second to consider the concept that something's "wrong" in your relationship. For instance, you may assume, "My spouse doesn't put a ton of effort into romance anymore. Our connection isn't nice and they don't love me." But when you look at reality, it's simple to point out all the ways they're compassionate and nice. Your ideas may not be congruent with what's going on and maybe what's producing unwarranted emotions of uncertainty.

9. You sense the chemistry

Even if you're experiencing a moment of uncertainty, assess if you still experience chemistry aka, that easy, breezy, flirtatious, fun optimism more often than not. This chemistry is an ethereal property that is frequently hard to evaluate. It's OK if you're going through a hard time. All couples do, at times. But if that chemistry is present, it's still more evidence you're a good fit.

10. Your doubt come and go

Consider if these doubts are transitory or whether they linger around. Too much probing might imply deeper flaws in the relationship. You'll want to follow your intuition and take a deeper look to find out why you feel the way you do. But if the uncertainty just creeps up once in a blue moon and doesn't feel particularly powerful, chances are you're doing OK.

11. You are appreciated

Keep an eye out every day as well as at instances when disrespect can be on full show, including during an argument, and ask yourself, "Do I feel safe? Do I feel respected?" If you don't feel any of them, you aren't with the appropriate person." Disrespect could appear like screaming, breaking limits, name-calling, lying, and the list goes on and on. You won't have to cope with any of these problems in a safe, healthy relationship.

12. Your lover is the first person you call

If you earn a promotion, acquire a dog, or just generally have a nice day, who's the first person you call? If it's your partner, then that's a positive indicator. The same is true with the negative items. If your spouse is one of the first people you call, it not only indicates you appreciate them but that they're a source of comfort.

13. You feel like the greatest version of yourself

Do you enjoy who you are around your partner? And do they urge you to be better? If they're content with who you are right now but also pump you up and help you attain your objectives, you've hit gold. The same is true in reverse. You adore who they are right now but also want to see them achieve, whether it's with a personal goal, a job objective, or elsewhere. You both encourage each other in becoming "better" and evolving into who you want to be as people.

14. Your pals are all about it

While you'll always want to trust your judgment of the relationship because you and your spouse are the only ones in it gaining an outside view might come in helpful, particularly if you're having second opinion. If well-intentioned persons like close friends and family are supportive and glad for you, you're likely with the correct person.

15. You enjoy their friendship

There is some validity to the adage that the people one chooses to surround oneself with speak a lot about a person. So, take a look at the individuals your spouse associates with, and analyze what it indicates. This doesn't mean you have to share interests with your significant other's pals, but they must be individuals you respect at a minimum and preferably someone you'd want to spend time with, too. If their buddies accept you into their circle with open arms, and vice versa, you've got a genuinely fantastic scenario on your hands.

16. You are both comfortable spending time alone

Taking time apart from your spouse and having areas of your own life that you partake in solo is important for a good relationship. Having hobbies and social engagements without our spouse enables us to acquire self-worth outside of our relationship, which is great for everyone involved. Not to mention, if you're both fine with spending time apart and can do it without it seeming like a huge issue, it indicates you have a strong degree of trust and respect for each other.

17. Everything appears fair and balanced

Making choices, completing tasks, and paying bills. Everything entails a mental strain, which is why you're likely with the correct person if they recognize it and do their part. You don't want it to seem like you're the only one doing the hard lifting, she adds, as it might lead to resentment. Instead, it should seem like you both show up 100 percent and take on these tasks jointly.

18. You are willing to work on the connection

Even though you're undoubtedly going through a challenging period, evaluate your attitude to it all. If you still feel ready to address concerns and strive toward specific solutions, it's an indication you still consider the relationship "worth it." You want to make things function because there's value. If you're still hesitant, though, speak to your spouse about your issues and anxieties. They need to know how you feel so they can join you in making great changes.

19. Your partner listens to you

If you and your partner can have a true discussion, feeding off each other's energy, and you realize that they're truly paying attention to every word coming out of your lips, you're with the appropriate person. This may seem unavoidable, but more often than not, it's simple for a partner to merely nod their head or shift the topic instead of listening and recognizing your remarks. Always monitor your partner as you talk: "Do they allow you to take the lead and not flip every topic back onto them? Do they recall what you have told them in the past?"

This shows that your partner cares about your opinions and is invested in engaging in healthy conversation with you.

20. They are happy about your personal growth

In a long-term relationship, you might experience professional, emotional, and physical changes that wouldn't just affect you, but your partner as well. Possibly you get a promotion, go to an entirely new job, or tick off a big life target of yours. If your spouse is genuinely joyful and excited about your success, then that's a positive signal that you're with the right spouse.

You can use your spouse's response to this personal growth as a way to decipher if you're truly well-matched. Otherwise, if you feel that your spouse is holding you back or not behind you, then that's a warning you could be in an unhealthy relationship.

21. You are not just in love, but in like as well

Sometimes knowing if you're with the correct person comes down not to how you equally express love, but how you express "like."

If you consider your partner one of your closest friends, or maybe even your best friend, it's more probable that you're with the proper person. Liking our spouse is highly undervalued, yet it's far easier to continue love when you really like each other as individuals and benefit from each other's company.

22. Acknowledge and respect your past trauma

One of the most important deciding factors when it comes to your relationship's future is whether or not they value your past traumas or negative experiences. Several of those recollections might still concern you to this day, and if your partner doesn't value that, it may mean they don't really know you. If you've adequately expressed these experiences to your spouse and they reply with a dismissing attitude, they're not your person. They should be aware of your anguish and demonstrate that they are capable of being the one who can sit in the agony with you, not attempt to repair you

23. Their words and deeds coincide

The proverb "actions speak louder than words" proved to be true here. If your spouse continues promising they'll take you out to dinner, or they'll fold the clothes in the dryer, or they'll prepare supper, but you have observed they're not following through with these statements, it might be a red sign. If your spouse is eager to make and remain loyalty with you, that's a green light.

24. You are learning from each other

Being in a relationship that actively teaches you new things can be extremely stimulating and it may well even be a deal breaker if it's not happening. If you're learning new opinions, new approaches, and new outlooks on life, you could observe that you're increasing into a more well-rounded side of yourself.

25. You know you can ask for space and receive it

Spending time apart indulging in various things is essential, but sometimes you simply need some time alone with yourself and your distinct ideas. Your spouse should recognize your own particular need for self-care and be ready to offer you the alone time you need.

When you are with the appropriate person, they will respect your time. Your spouse should realize that personal self-care time is vital to being a better version of yourself. Whether you need to take an hour-long bath or go on a stroll by yourself, your spouse should accept that and allow you adequate space.

26. You both respect each other's love language

Every individual has a distinct connection with the five love languages; a word of affirmation, gift giving, quality time, acts of service, and physical contact. Each individual will receive and give forth love in various ways. Knowing your partner’s and your love languages can be immensely effective in a romantic relationship.

27. Your lover doesn’t attempt to modify you

If you believe you have stayed real and true to who you are as a person throughout your whole relationship, this is certainly a green light. The appropriate person accepts you for who you are, with all of your faults and failings. Your spouse does assist you to see where you're wrong, but they don’t urge you to modify your routines to satisfy them or their lifestyle.

28. They establish the connection in the least intimate moment

Feeling romantically connected to your partner can happen in other moments besides sex. Intimacy may be developed via dialogue, intelligence, and emotional connection. Intimacy is about a real mind, body, and soul connection that spreads throughout your body like an electrical charge, even when merely preparing dinner or conversing on the phone on your way home from work. Emotional closeness is a genuine phenomenon.

29. You are both devoted to the relationship

Relationship dynamics alter with time. "The phase of the first animalistic connection will pass and your relationship will change through time. If your spouse is still as dedicated to your relationship as they were in the very beginning, you're with the correct one. You both sincerely want to make the marriage work.

30. You could live with this person as they are now

If you're telling yourself, "one day they'll change," your spouse is not the person you're supposed to be with. It's so easy to slip into the trap of thinking that with the correct influence, the other person's peculiarities and defects would smooth out. If you can't see being in a relationship with this person a few years down the road precisely the way they are now, it's time to re-evaluate your options. Imagine moving in with your lover tomorrow. Could you do it? If you could, that's a wonderful indication.

Chapter 7

What Your Body Language Says About Your Relationship

Our communication is made up of both verbal and non-verbal signs. From our facial expressions to how we posture our body, the things we don't say nonetheless convey a message and affect how we interact with others. When we acquaint ourselves with body language, we get better at comprehending what people convey without using words. Awareness of body language indicators also helps our communication abilities. Through the command of our body language cues, we are managing the message we are giving out and lowering the possibility of conveying something we never meant to "say."

Before we continue to give instances of body language cues, let's establish what body language is first.

What is body language?

Body language refers to the non-verbal component of communication. A major amount of communication consists of non-verbal signs, including body language. According to research, that section represents 60-65 percent of our everyday contacts. Other kinds of non-verbal communication include facial expressions, appearance, touch, eye contact, personal space, gestures, paralinguistics like the tone of voice, and artifacts such as objects and photographs. Reading body language begins with grasping the meaning of the body language cues. Although the interpretation of body language signals may fluctuate based on the context and persons involved, certain indications are more plain and evident in their meaning.

Positive body language indicators

1. Smiling

We have 43 muscles on our face; therefore it's no surprise that the face is our most exposed body part. Think about how much a person can communicate with their facial expression.

If someone says to you they are OK, but their face doesn’t portray the proper emotion, you won’t trust what they are saying. Also, we form the judgment on their emotional health and personality unbelievably rapidly. Data suggested that 100 ms exposure to a face is adequate for individuals to develop numerous personal judgments such as trustworthiness, competency, and aggression.

Interestingly, they also observed that the facial expression combining a modest lift of the eyebrows and a slight grin is most connected to friendliness and confidence. Therefore, smiling endures as one of the most essential positive body language indicators.

2. Mimicking each other’s motions

Body language of couples that are blissfully in love reveals they tend to move, smile, and talk similarly. Spending a lot of time together and finding someone appealing causes us to, mainly unconsciously, copy their behaviors. Mirroring one other’s actions is considered the body language of couples in love.

3. Synchronized walking

Couples' body language displays how much they are intimate and linked via indications such as how in tune they are with one other while strolling, for instance. The more they are aware and connected to their partner's non-verbal cues, the more they can mirror their walking style. Therefore, we might infer that the amount of intimacy will affect the synchrony of partners' activities.

4. Body inclined toward each other

There is one body language secret, everybody, trying to know whether a person likes them should know. When we find someone intriguing or exciting, our body instinctively bends toward them. We are not even aware of when this occurs. Therefore, you may use this body language indication to assess how the other person feels about you. Does their body or tips of legs point towards you? Keep an eye out for this body language of affection.

5. Spontaneous and frequent touching

When we feel attracted to someone, we want to touch them almost automatically. Whether it is removing the "evident" dust bunnies off their shirt, a delicate stroking on the arm, or a spontaneous touch while conversing, this body language indicator communicates a desire for intimacy When there is an emotional connection, touching is as natural as breathing.

6. Leaning toward each other

If you are wanting to grasp relationship body language, keep an eye out for persons inclining themselves to be closed near the other person. Are they leaning in while the other is talking? Leaning the upper body towards someone and aligning our face with theirs is a show of real attention. Furthermore, putting your head on someone's shoulder as a relationship, body language correlates with trust and connection. This suggests you are comfortable being physically near to them, and it speaks to closeness in the relationship.

7. Gazing into each other's eyes

There are a reason people say "eyes are a mirror of the soul." So much may be absorbed in one glance. Eye contact love signals may convey in them a complete speech. Therefore, when someone is gazing at you regularly or staring into your eyes a little longer than normal, you may be quite confident they are interested in you. Furthermore, couples who are close and in love may exchange complete conversations with only one glance. They naturally glance at each other when anything is occurring to check for their loved one's responses.

Therefore, eye contact and love signals signify trust, familiarity, and mutual understanding that doesn't require words.

8. Open palms during a chat

Our posture and gestures alter based on our opinion of the person and our dialogues because our bodies represent how we feel.

Hence, when we are interested in what someone is saying to us and eager to listen to the other, our hands generally show it via movements of openness. Exposed hands are typically a sign of an open mind and undivided attention to a person.

9. Protective gestures

Have you observed a partner put their arm around you in public to protect you? Perhaps they grab your hand naturally while crossing the street? Do they notice if someone is making you uncomfortable and enter the discussion to defend you?

Actions like this reveal they wish to protect you like we all do when we care for someone. They naturally need to make sure you are secure.

10. Special rites specific to you two

Do you have a special way you high-five each other, wink, or say goodbye to each other? Just like internal jokes, private handshakes, and particular rituals testify to the depth of your familiarity. When we know one other well and feel connected, it reflects in our actions.

Conclusion

Learning how to communicate is vital for couples who wish to address marital issues without hurting one other's emotions.

The cornerstones of successful communication include learning to listen, keeping courteous, attempting to view a problem from your partner's perspective, and forgiving each other. These suggestions will help you handle your disagreements without starting a conflict.

www.ingramcontent.com/pod-product-compliance
Lightning Source LLC
LaVergne TN
LVHW050339160826
845677LV00014B/3686

9798844316623